THE

GRAND DUCHESS

OF GEROLSTEIN.

COMIC OPERA IN THREE ACTS,

BY

HENRY MEILHAC and LUDOVIC HALEVY.

The Music by J. Offenbach.

AS PERFORMED BY THE

Soldene English Opera Bouffe Company,

AT THE LYCEUM THEATRE, NEW YORK,

UNDER THE MANAGEMENT OF

MESSRS. MAURICE GRAU and C. A. CHIZZOLA.

———•◆•———

New York:
METROPOLITAN PRINTING AND ENGRAVING ESTABLISHMENT,
HERALD BUILDING, BROADWAY AND ANN STREET.
1876.

In the interest of creating a more extensive selection of rare historical book reprints, we have chosen to reproduce this title even though it may possibly have occasional imperfections such as missing and blurred pages, missing text, poor pictures, markings, dark backgrounds and other reproduction issues beyond our control. Because this work is culturally important, we have made it available as a part of our commitment to protecting, preserving and promoting the world's literature. Thank you for your understanding.

CHARACTERS.

GRAND DUCHESS............Miss EMILY SOLDENE
WANDA, a Peasant Girl....................Miss CLARA VESEY
PRINCE PAUL...................................Mr. J. B. RAE
GENERAL BOOM, Commander-in-Chief............Mr. E. LEWENS
BARON PUCK, a Diplomatist....................Mr. E. MARSHALL
BARON GROG, a Diplomatist....................Mr. F. CHARLES
NEPOMUC, Aide-de-Camp to the Grand Duchess...Mr J. WALLACE
FRITZ, a Soldier.............................Mr. BEVERLEY

Ladies of the Court, Maids of Honor, Pages, Soldiers of the Grand Duchess' Army, Vivandieres, &c.

DIRECTRESS......................................Miss EMILY SOLDENE

THE GRAND DUCHESS
OF
GEROLSTEIN.

ACT I.

SCENE I.—*An encampment of soldiers. Soldiers, peasants, girls, vivandieres.*

CHORUS.

Ere call'd to face the foeman's volley,
And rush to death or victory,
We'll quaff and laugh—short life and jolly
The soldier's maxim aye should be:
Laughing,
Quaffing,
Dancing,
Prancing,
Ere call'd to face the foeman's volley,
And rush to death or victory, &c.

Enter FRITZ *and* WANDA.

WANDA. Sad, dear Fritz, am I at learning
To the wars that you must go.
FRITZ. Dear, to hasten my returning,
I'll the deuce play with the foe.

SONG.

1.

Round in circles spinning,
Twirl ye maidens free;
Soon you homeward hieing
Sheltered all will be,
While howe'er unwilling,
Off we chaps must trot,
For a paltry shilling
Standing to be shot.
But what boots complaining,
Fate we can't withstand!
So the time remaining
Pass we glass in hand.

Off the tankard toss, then,
   Each man's lot is cast.
Your's, dear, were the loss, then,
   Prov'd this cup the last.
Come maidens so winning,
   Brave lads all, and some
To waltz hither come
   With fife and with drum,
Like a top round spinning,
   Or a te-to-tum.
To waltz hither come
   With fife and with drum.

II.

When the trumpet sounding
   Summons us to march,
Tears and sobs abounding,
   Pretty throats will parch.
Calm your apprehension,
   Dears, we'll write anon,
And correctly mention
   How we'er getting on.
Thus all fears allaying,
   Hearts will constant prove,
Though away we're staying,
   But till off we'll move
Down the wine we'll toss, dears,
   Arms about you cast.
Yours would be the loss, dears,
   Prov'd this kiss the last.
Come each maiden arming
   Brave lads all, and some
To waltz hither come
   With fife and with drum,
Like a top round spinning,
   Or a te-to-tum.
To waltz hither come
   With fife and with drum.

Enter GENERAL BOOM.

GEN. BOOM. What! women in the camp? 'Tis no less than flat treason
FRITZ. Jove! 'Tis he! What a start!
GEN. BOOM Have you then lost, my men, all sense of time and season?
FRITZ. A soldier tho' he be a man has still a heart.
GEN BOOM. You again! dare wag your tongue?
FRITZ. I only said—
GEN. BOOM.   Don't reason!
   Whene'er I frown to speak none dare,
   That I ne'er joke all are aware.

CHORUS.

Whene'er he frowns, to speak none dare
That he ne'er jokes all are aware.

SONG.—GEN. BOOM.

Never balked—never hesitating—
   Onward I swoop!
O'er hill and dale exterminating
   Troop after troop!
The fiercest foe that moment cowers.
   Quaking with dread,
When he beholds this plume that towers
   Here o'er my head.
With a bing, bang bong, ta-ta-ra-pa-poom!
A General am I and my name is Boom!

CHORUS

With a bing, bang, bong, ta-ta-ra-pa-poom!
A General is he and his name is Boom!

II.

And when the din of battle o'er
  Home I repair,
In festive halls I'm for a lover
  Claimed by each one fair;
While my Moustache they stroke confessing
  Me they adore.
I own my plume gets quite distressing—
  In fact a bore!
With a bing, bang, bong, ta-ta-ra-pa-poom!
  A General am I and my name is Boom!

CHORUS.

With a bing, bang, bong, ta-ta-ra-pa-poom!
A General is he and his name is Boom!

ALL. Hurrah! for General Boom!
BOOM. That's my brave fellows. Now I recognize the gallant soldiers of our sovereign mistress, the Grand Duchess of Gerolstein.
ALL. Long live the Grand Duchess!
BOOM. You're not a bad lot of soldiers, but that fellow Fritz there sets you a shocking example.
FRITZ. There now! I knew he'd come down upon me.
BOOM. Private Fritz! step forward!
FRITZ. General—
BOOM. You're a disgrace to the service.
FRITZ. Ah! I know what makes you go on like that, it all comes of the girls.
BOOM. What do you mean, sir?
FRITZ. That you are making up to little Wanda.
BOOM. No such thing.
FRITZ. I beg your pardon, you did make up to her, and she would'nt have you, seeing that she's in love with me, and that's how it is.
BOOM. (*aside*). Furies.
FRITZ. Women have such very bad taste. They actually prefer a young soldier to the venerable commander.
BOOM. I'll have you sent to the black hole.
FRITZ. That won't alter the case.
BOOM. I'll have you shot.
FRITZ. Oh! that would be clever!
BOOM. You're a disgrace to the service!
FRITZ. Much you'd care if I was; on the contrary, I'm a very pretty soldier, and that's what makes you mad.
BOOM. Silence!
FRITZ. Oh! I'm dumb, but never mind,
BOOM. I never paid the slightest attention to the young woman.
FRITZ. Begging your pardon a second time, you did pay her a great deal of attention.

Enter NEPOMUC.

NEP. General!
BOOM. (*eagerly*). Let me hope, sir, you come to announce the enemy's approach—say so, sir—I entreat you to say so!
NEP. No, General. I have merely come to inform you that the Grand Duchess is coming to inspect her regiment.
BOOM. Soldiers! you hear.
NEP. She desires that a tent may be erected for her—on this spot—in the very midst of her soldier's encampment. [*Exit* R. U. E.]
BOOM. Sharp! there—post a sentry here!—private Fritz?
FRITZ (*aside*), He always pitches on me—(*aloud*) General—
BOOM. You'll mount guard here.
FRITZ. Of course, right under the blazing sun.

Boom. No remarks!
Fritz. What on earth is the use of a sentry there?
Boom. To keep guard over the Grand Duchess's tent.
Fritz. Well, but there's no tent up yet.
Boom. You'll keep guard over the spot where it is to be.
Fritz. I suppose then it's to prevent some one from running away with the groun
Why there's no sense at all in it.
Boom. You're always supposing *then*.
Fritz. Very good—very good—I know what it all means—it's all the girls—th
what it is—all the girls.
Boom. Oh, wouldn't I have you shot, my fine fellow, but that on the eve of a ba
I dare not diminish my effective force.
Fritz. Ah, that's where it is—you're afraid to diminish your effective force.
Boom. Then I'm not to have the last word?
Fritz. Why, of course not.
Boom. In that case I shan't be such an ass as to hold out, Soldiers, form.
Fritz. Now I should very much like to know where the deuce you are off to no
Boom. By the Lord, this is too much. What business is that of yours? Am I
ing to be called upon to give you an account of all my movements? Soldiers! to
left wheel! forward, march!

CHORUS.

With a bing, bang, bong—tara-pa-pa-pa-poom
Our General leads on, follow we, Boom, Boom.

Exeunt soldiers.

Boom. Ugh! a disgrace to the service. [*Exi*
Fritz (*alone*). That's another clever trick, coming and making faces at a poor you
soldier, who can't answer his general. I declare I can't understand some things.
see a lot of generals, with all sorts of promotions and honors, fancying that's all th
want to please the women. Not a bit of it. It turns out they prefer the young sold
with no promotion at all, but a pleasant way with him. So the old general begins
badger the young soldier; and that's how it is, and that's how it will be to the end
the chapter—and all along of the girls—and nothing else. Ah, here she comes—he
comes little Wanda. She thought I was coming after her—I wish I could—and see
that I didn't she's coming after me. Here she comes (*Enter* Wanda); oh, would
not rile the general to see this now.

DUO. Wanda *and* Fritz.

Wanda. Here am I, Fritz—I've come so fast
That I declare I feel quite flurried.
But by those stern looks on me cast
Twould seem I need not thus have hurried.
Say why?

Reply.

Pray, what mean, sir, those airs displeasing,
I hither haste and find you freezing.
Say are you dumb, bold Grenadier,
And must, by signs, hold conversation?

Fritz.

I must obey the regulation,
On guard a sentry's voice none may hear.

Wanda.

Cease this nonsense, or dread a scolding.
Your future spouse, sir, when beholding
All other thoughts should disappear.
Speak! ere you feel my indignation.

FRITZ.

I can't, indeed—the regulation
Bids me not budge one step from here.

ENSEMBLE.

I can't, indeed—the regulation, &c., &c.

WANDA.

He answers no—the regulation
Bids him not budge one step from there.
[FRITZ crosses R.]
What if with tender glance appealing,
I said—"Awhile before me kneeling,
To breathe thy love come hither dear?"
Would you say no?

FRITZ.

The regulation
Forbids me budge one step from here.

WANDA.

But say, made wildly fond by Cupid,
I should exclaim—"You dear old stupid,
Come kiss me quick, and go, my dear."
Would you dare slight my invitation?

FRITZ.

Not I, indeed—the regulation
'Gainst kissing has no rule severe.

WANDA.

I could have sworn the regulation
'Gainst kissing had no rule severe.

ENSEMBLE.

Oh! hang the regulation,
And heigh! then, for love,
Spite of rule and regulation,
We'ell no master have but love.

FRITZ.

Don't you think, having once begone, dear,
'Twere well to return to the cheer.

WANDA.

One kiss, I said—enough of one, dear;
Not two—that might strange appear.

FRITZ.

Just one wee kiss—

WANDA.

Learn moderation!
No, no.
The regulation
Against kissing is severe.

ENSEMBLE.

Oh! hang the regulation,
And heigh! then, for love,
Spite of rule and regulation,
We'll no master have but love.

[*Enter* GEN. BOOM.

BOOM. Ha! I've caught you, have I.
FRITZ (*aside.*) We're in for it!
WANDA. Oh! Fritz, dear.
BOOM. My orders to you to keep guard here, the movement I caused my army to execute, all was done to catch you out, and I have caught you out.
FRITZ. Well, now you ought to feel quite pleased, for it's the first time I ever knew any of your movements come to anything.
BOOM. Scoundrel (*report of a gun.*)
WANDA. Ah!
FRITZ. Dearest Wanda!
BOOM. What's that! I demand to know what that is?
FRITZ. An attack of the enemy, perhaps. Won't you let me carry her back to her mother.

(*A second report is heard.*)

BOOM. Go—quick—and take great care of her.
FRITZ. There now, General, arn't it clear; now arn't it clear you're fond of her?
BOOM. Go, sir, go.
FRITZ. Come along, dearest, and have a little drop of Schnaps. (*Exeunt. The report of firearms is again repeated y heard. Enter* BARON PUCK.
PUCK. Oh, Boom, my dear friend!
BOOM. What has happened?
PUCK. Challenged by the sentry, and being absorbed in profound political combinations, I neglected giving the pass-word, and so—
BOOM. Bang, bang, bing, bong!
PUCK. Bang, bang, bing, bong—they fired.
BOOM. It was their duty.
PUCK. Fortunately they missed.
BOOM. For that they shall be punished.
PUCK. What!
BOOM. I say they ought not to have missed you.
PUCK. Why, you wouldn't have had them—
BOOM. Speaking as a commanding officer, certainly—as a friend it would have pained me.
PUCK. Thank you.
BOOM. May I ask to what I am indebted for the honor of—
PUCK. A very delicate affair. You are aware it is our custom on the eve of a battle to neglect no means to spirit up the troops and rouse their enthusiasm.
BOOM. Just so.
PUCK. This time we have hit upon a device which I flatter myself is sufficiently ingenious. The Grand Duchess is coming.
BOOM. I know it.
PUCK. She will stand here in the midst of her soldiers, and you will then offer to have the song of the regiment sung before her.
BOOM. Good.
PUCK. Her Highness will reply, "I know the song well," and then she'll sing it.
BOOM. Herself?
PUCK. Herself. And you, Rudolph, will take the second.
BOOM. I! what an honor; but does she really know it?
PUCK. Perfectly; we rehearsed it for two hours this very morning.
BOOM. Good! It's a settled affair, then?
PUCK. Quite. Now for a word or two on our own private affairs. Do you do anything in this line?
BOOM. Not with that stuff; that's my mixture!
PUCK. You know why we are going to war?
BOOM. I? Not an atom.
PUCK. Then I'll tell you. The Grand Duchess, our Sovereign, and my pupil—for I have been her precepter. Graitous Heaven! look there!
BOOM. What is it?
PUCK. Look—look—a bullet hole!
BOOM. Come, that wasn't such a bad shot.

PUCK. It's given me such a turn. What a blessing I had my hat on—I should ave been a dead man.
BOOM. Put it on again directly.
PUCK. Ah true, they might fire again Well, the Grand Duchess, our sovereign nd my pupil, is in her twentieth year. Up to the present time she has left the ower of the state in our hands, but of late I have observed about her certain tokens of neasiness—of preoccupation. Said I, "That young person is beginning to feel bored ith existance, her mind must be diverted, I declared war, and there you have it.
BOOM. Ingenious—very!
PUCK. Eh? Divert the mind has always been my maxim in dealing with my pupil. irst with toys when she was a child; later other means had to be devised. It was to vert her mind that I sought her a husband.
BOOM. Prince Paul?
PUCK. Precisely: but that unhappy Prince produced no impression. True, I lected him on account of his utter harmlessness. For six months she has kept him angling. Last week his father, the Elector of Steis-Stein-Steis Langen-Hosen Schor- enburg charged one of his principle officers, Baron Grog, with a mission to persuade ir amiable sovereign to pronounce the desired affirmative. Our amiable sover- gn distinctly refused to receive Baron Grog, and she continues to feel life a bore. et us hope that war will cheer up her spirits.
BOOM. Rely on me for that.
PUCK. Unfortunately that resource will soon be exhausted. The Princess is in er twentieth year; she will discover that the world has other pleasures, her heart is atheless as yet, but who knows how long it may remain so.
BOOM. You alarm me!
PUCK. Have you ever reflected on our probable fate were the Grand Duchess to se her heart to some gay gallant?
BOOM. We should be nowhere. That must be prevented.
PUCK It must!
BOOM. It must! (*Drums heard at some distance. Enter* NEPOMUC.) The enemy? ay is it the enemy?
NEPO. It is not the enemy, General, but her Highness who is approaching.
BOOM. 'Tis well, sir; order the troops under arms.
NEPO. Yes, General. [*Exit.*
PUCK You understand our plans, lull her to-day with the charms of the regimental ng, a week hence dazzle her with the glories of victory.
BOOM. Then return to our hearths and homes.
PUCK. And share the power of the State.
BOOM. And share the power of the State.
Enter the GRAND DUCHESS *with her maids of honor,* IZA, OLGA, AMELIA, *and* CHAR- OTTE *and* NEPOMUC *with the staff of the* GRAND DUCHESS.

CHORUS.

    Carry arms, present arms,
    Eyes right, attention there:
    None in grace and beauty's charms,
    With our Grand Duchess can compare;
    Carry arms! Present arms!

RONDO.

GRAND D.   Ah! I doat on the military,
    With their uniforms so bright,
    Their moustaches and trappings light.
    Ah! I doat on the military,
    Their dauntless mein; their manners airy;
    In all I delight!

    When I view my troopers rare,
    With martial fire animated,
    Eyes right, right attention there!
    By Jove! with pride I'm all elated,
    Whether or not they'll thrash the foe
    I cannot tell, but this I know.

CHORUS.

    But this she knows

GRAND D.   This I know,
                    That I doat on the military, &c.

                    Could I have my little way
                    I'd enlist as a vivandiére,
                    Their wants tending all the day,
                    With drink I'd make them gay!
                    Then brave as steel and light as air,
                    To the fight I'd march away,
                    If war would seem such fun when there,
                    I cannot tell, but this I'll say,
CHORUS.   This she'll say,
GRAND D.   Yes, this I'll say,
                    That I doat on the military, &c., &c.

THE ARMY. Hurrah for the Grand Duchess.
GRAND D. (*To Boom.*) General, I am gratified, highly gratified, General.
BOOM. Your Highness.
GRAND D. Let that soldier step forward.
BOOM. Schwarz.
GRAND D. No, not that one, not Schwarz.
BOOM. Schumaker.
GRAND D. No, not Schumaker, the other. Now you're right.
BOOM. Private Fritz—three paces forward.
GRAND D. What is your name?
FRITZ. Fritz.
GRAND D. Name your campaigns—the number and nature of your wounds.
FRITZ. No campaigns—no wounds—yes, once climbing over a wall to get at som apples I slightly—but I suppose that don't count—no—no wounds.
GRAND D. You are only a private?
FRITZ. Only a private.
GRAND D. I promote you to be a corporal.
FRITZ. A corporal.
BOOM. Hallo! Thunder and ouns!
FRITZ. Very good—very good.
GRAND D. Where are you going, my man.
FRITZ. To tell my young woman I was made a corporal.
GRAND D. Oh, indeed! Well—
BOOM. Well?
GRAND D. You may tell your young woman then that you are a sergeant. (*To Boo* Give the word to dismiss, General.
BOOM. Dismiss! And be off with you.
GRAND D. Why should they be off. Are they not my soldiers—my children?
PUCK. Capital! your Highness, capital!
GRAND D. Stay here, my friends, and let us have a friendly gossip.
PUCK (*to* BOOM). Did you observe the marked way in which her Highness fix her gaze on that soldier?
BOOM. I did, but you can't of course suppose—
PUCK. We are to suppose everything. As her Highnesses's preceptor I allow her to get into the habit of pleasing herself in everything
BOOM. The deuce you did;—then we must keep our eye on her.
PUCK. We must.
GRAND D. (*to* FRITZ. Come a little nearer, my man.
FRITZ. Your Highness.
PUCK (*to* BOOM). There, there she goes again.
BOOM (*to* PUCK). I observe; as for you, I'll be one with you before long.
GRAND D. And is your young woman pleased at your promotion?
FRITZ. Delighted.
GRAND D. And you—and your comrades—are you contented?
FRITZ. Well, you see your Highness, that's according—a man's contented and isn't—that's nature.
GRAND D. Well fed.
FRITZ. Well—yes—not bad—plenty of potatoes—pretty well fed, though all t same.
GRAND D. Officers behave well to their men?
FRITZ. Yes, the officers are very well, some good and some bad; but the general he does come down hard on us.
GRAND D. Indeed?
BOOM. Your Highness—

GRAND. D. Let the man speak.
FRITZ. He does come down hard does the general—but I know why—it's all along of the girls—that's what it is.
GRAND D. How so?
BOOM. I really can't allow—
GRAND D. General Boom, I desire you to let the man speak. You were saying, my man?
FRITZ. General's very hard—because he made up to my young woman and she sent him about his business.
GRAND D. Bless me—why every one seems in love with your young woman? Is she so very pretty then?
FRITZ. There is the party herself a standing out there.
GRAND D. Call her hither.
FRITZ. Here, Wanda. She's shy, you see. Come along. They're tiresome creatures not like us young soldiers.
GRAND D. And so this great tall fellow loves you, eh?
WANDA. I think so.
GRAND D. And you love him?
WANDA. Oh, that I am sure of.
GRAND D. Indeed! *(Aside.)* Bless me! I never felt like this before. *(To FRITZ.)* Did I inform you, that you were a lieutenant?
FRITZ. No, your Highness.
GRAND D. Well, now I inform you of it.
FRITZ. And I say much obliged.
PUCK *(to BOOM).* She's going a pretty pace?
BOOM *(to PUCK).* Don't fret. To-morrow I'll put that lieutenant well in front of the battle.
GRAND D. The heat is very oppressive. Ladies, would'nt you like something to quench your thirst?
IZA. That we should, your highness.
GRAND D. And so should I.
PUCK. Quick, some lemonade—ices.
GRAND D. Lemonade! ices!—nonsense—I wish to drink what my soldiers drink.
BOOM. But your Highness, they drink—
GRAND D. What the canteen woman pours out for them, I suppose. This way vivandiere, and pour me out a glass—fill to the brim! Soldiers! here's victory, and a speedy return!
ALL. Long live the Grand Duchess.
PUCK *(to BOOM).* My pupil's getting on.
BOOM *(to PUCK).* I think now she's about ripe for the song.
PUCK. You're right.
BOOM. As your Highness has condescended to beguile a few moments among your faithful troops, perhaps your Highness might not object to hear the regimental song?
GRAND D. Ah, a good thought. General, the song is one I know well.
BOOM. Indeed your Highness.
GRAND D. And if you've no objection I'll sing it myself.
BOOM. Oh, your Highness.
GRAND D. We'll strike up at once.
BOOM. La, la, la!
GRAND D. Are you going to sing it with me?
BOOM. If your Highness will condescend to allow me.
GRAND D. You, a general-in-chief! Out of the question! It would ruin your authority. *(To FRITZ.)* Come here, my man—you shall sing it with me.
BOOM. Surely your Highness will not—
GRAND D. I beg your pardon—
BOOM. A mere lieutenant sing with—
GRAND D. If the rank of lieutenant is too humble, I make him a captain. Is that high enough?
GRAND D. This way, gallant captain; and we will sing together.

THE REGIMENTAL SONG.

I.

GRAND D.

Oh! what a gallant reg-i-ment
Is this regiment—the Grand Duchess's own!

Fritz.

When'er to catch the foe theyr'e sen
On their nobs don't they just rattle down.

Grand D.

Some say the Hussars ain't so bad
And show more than one tidy lad.

Fritz.

With 's 'elmet of steel polished bright
The *drag*-oon makes a *purty* sight.

Grand D.

All know in the Artilleree
Brave boys you as any may see.

Fritz.

But none can e'en a rushlight hold
To the reg-i-ment you now behold.
     Whack-row-de-dow !

Grand D.

Whack row-de-dow-row-de-dow—
     How *are* you now ?

Ensemble.

Then let the drums all rattle
 And let all the trumpets ring ;
We'll sing the God of battles,
 The God of Love we'll sing.

Grand D.

Oh, what a gallant reg-i-ment
Is this regiment—the Grand Duchess's own.

Fritz.

By honor rul'd in sentiment
Its lass as Victory by name is known.

Grand D.

Where'er its standard proud 's unfurled
In any quarter of the world.

Fritz.

It makes the girls all beam with smiles,
The men it howsomedever riles,

Grand D.

But when again they're all en route
On t'other leg you find the boot,

Fritz.

It makes the men all beam with smiles
The girls it howsomedever riles,

ENSEMBLE.

Then let the drums all rattle.

Enter NEPOMUC.

NEPO. Your Highness—your Highness.
GRAND D. Well, what's the matter?
BOOM. I hope this time at least, Sir, you have come to announce the enemy.
NEPO. I wish you wouldn't always say that. (*To the* GRAND DUCHESS). Prince Paul your Highness has advanced as far as the outposts, accompanied by Baron Grog, and desires to be furnished with the pass-word that he may reach your Highness.
GRAND D. Prince Paul—what again!
NEPO. What answer shall I give?
GRAND D. Oh—there—go and fetch Prince Paul, and bring him here. As for the Baron Grog, I don't want to hear of him. I have refused to receive him, and receive him, I shall not. (NEPOMUC *exit*.) Gallant captain away and return in your uniform. I want to see how you will look in it.
FRITZ. I shall look superb! [*Exit.*]
GRAND D. (*To the soldiers*.) Now my men you may go. By-and-by I shall see you again for the last time before you repair to the field of battle
GRAND D. My worthy preceptor, remain within call, and you too general. Presently we will examine your plan of operation.
BOOM. Your Highness will find it without a flaw.
GRAND D. I am willing to believe so Go until I send for you. Prince Paul! now he's grown more insupportable to me than ever.
PRINCE P. Well your highness this is not the happy day yet.
GRAND D. Why, Prince, what is the meaning of that costume?
PRINCE P. Ah! you have deigned to notice it. It is the costume of a bridegroom, I put it on thinking it might move you to make up your mind.
GRAND D. What! to marry you to day? Impossible, my dear Prince. I've too much on my hands—a plan of military operations to settle, an army on the point of departure—impossible I can ever find time to get married.
PRINCE P. Your Highness is never at a loss for excellent reasons.
GRAND D. Well, you admit they are excellent?
PRINCE P. Yes, but for six months I've had nothing else, I've lived on excellent reasons, and this morning Baron Grog, that worthy but rejected messenger of love, has received a letter from Papa.
GRAND D. And what says your papa in that letter?
PRINCE P. He says he's nearly had enough of it. It's six months since I left to get married, all of which time he's made me a handsome allowance, and all of which time I've spent my allowance and never married anybody. So the old gentleman says he's had enough of it and wants to know how it's to end.
GRAND D. Does he, indeed?
PRINCE P. Yes, because if it's not to come off with you, he could turn me on to another Grand Duchess.
GRAND D. Make the Elector's mind easy, the marriage is sure to come off—one of these fine days.
PRINCE P. That's what you always say. My marriage has been announced to all the foreign courts; the world has its eye upon me and no doubt begins to think I cut a very ridiculous figure.
GRAND D. Well, to be sure, if the world has its eye upon you at this particular minute—
PRINCE P. Yes, and there's another thing that hurts my feelings even more.
GRAND D.—What in the world may that be?
PRINCE P. Look there!
GRAND D. What's this?
PRINCE P.—A newspaper printed at Hamburgh in which my name is mentioned.
GRAND D. You don't say so.
PRINCE P. Positively, it's a fact. A set of scoundrelly fellows have sprung up who take upon themselves to write and publish all sorts of things about every thing and everybody in what they call journals, and people call them journalists, and monstrous to relate they not only go into public matters, but into the private life of individuals and what's worse than all they have gone into my private life. Just listen to this now:

"To wed the Pearl of Princesses,
Prince Paul set forth upon his way.
But it would seem that nothing presses,
The wedding's for another day.

Now ev'ry morning, ere 'tis light yet,
   Prince Paul puts on the whitest kids.
"Is it to day?" "Oh, no, not quite yet."
   Of gloves the Prince his hands then rids.
Prince Paul's endurance seems eternal.
   He pines—but breathes not yea or nay."
Of me that's what these fellows say
   In that confounded Hamburgh journal.

GRAND D.

Ferm thru'h they're never wide astray,
   Those writers in the Hamburgh journal.

PRINCE P. Oh! but that's not all, there some more.

II.

"The Prince was quite an ardent lover.
   To woo this Princess when he came,
The Prince with love was all a-flame,
   So fierce his flame, to put it mildly,
Since now six months, or thereabouts,
   His passion has been blazing wildly,
It surely now must be burnt out.
   Prince Paul, take this advice paternal.
Pack up and homeward wend your way."
Of me that's what these fellows say
   In that confounded Hamburgh journal.

GRAND D.

From truth they're never wide astray,
   Those writers in the Hamburgh journal.

PRINCE P. Now's it's very wicked of you to laugh.

Enter FRITZ.

FRITZ. Here I am according to orders.
GRAND D. Oh! I vow it sets him off wonderfully! (*To* PRINCE PAUL.) Look at him, Prince, and tell me what you think of him.
PRINCE P. A well-limbed fellow, egad!
GRAND D. Is it not a proud thing to command men such as that? (*to* FRITZ) Gallant Captain?
FRITZ. Your Highness.
GRAND D. Enter that tent and inform General Boom and Baron Puck that we await their presence.
FRITZ. Well, I've no objection.
PRINCE P. Your Highness.
GRAND D. Again! What now?
PRINCE P. You haven't given me an answer.
GRAND D. What answer can I give you? The very first occasion the cares of government leave me one moment to bestow on the thought of my future happiness, I shall avail myself of it to marry you. Until then I recommend your patience.
PRINCE P. That's the way I'm continually fubbed off.

Enter GENERAL BOOM, BARON PUCK, *and* FRITZ.

GRAND D. We are about to examine General Boom's plan of operations. (*To* PRINCE PAUL.) May we hope, prince, you will enlighten us with your observations?
PRINCE P. Oh! if you wish it.
GRAND D. What! cross? Oh naughty!
PRINCE P. It's because you always make me stop while you're holding council.
GRAND D. And isn't it quite natural? As my future consort are you not entitled to all the privileges—?
PRINCE P. No, you don't refuse me any of the political privileges of my position, but there are others—
GRAND D. Pray what is your meaning, Prince?
PRINCE P. (*aside.*) There, now, I'm silenced—hang my confounded timidity.
GRAND D. Gentlemen, be seated. Captain you will guard our person.

Fritz. Let any one touch you, that's all!
Boom. Really, I don't know whether I ought to develop my plans—
Grand D. Don't trouble yourself about that, general, but proceed.
Boom. Nothing can be more simple your Highness. You see the art of war may be summed up in two words—to cut off and to wrap up—
Grand D. Like a slice of plum cake then?
Boom. Precisely, your Highness. Now in order to enable me to cut off and wrap up, this is what I do—I divide my army into three corps.
Puck. Good!
Boom. One will push forward to the right.
Paul. Good!
Boom. Another to the left.
Puck. Good!
Boom. And the third in the middle.
Paul. Good!
Boom. Thus disposed, my forces will proceed by three different routes to one central point upon which I have decided to concentrate them. Now, where that point is to be I don't know, but what I know is that I shall thrash the enemy, thrash them soundly!
Grand D. Pray contain yourself.
Puck. General, I entreat you.
Boom. I tell you I'll thrash them soundly!
Grand D. I don't say you won't; but you will do yourself some injury.
Boom. It's for my country's sake. The enemy! Where's the enemy? Lead me to the enemy!
Fritz. Aren't you going to meet him presently, general, and by three different routes?
Puck. Hold your tongue, sir.
Fritz. Three routes! Three routes! Three routes! What a delicious joke!
Boom. What's that he says?
Fritz. Three routes! Why it's downright tomfoolery!
Prince P. Well, I never!
Boom. I'll have you shot, sir!
Puck. Use such language to the general!
Grand D. One moment's silence, if you please, gentlemen. (*To* Fritz.) You were observing, I think, captain, that General Boom's plan was downright tomfoolery.
Fritz. Of course, and I'll prove it.
Puck. Allow me respectfully to submit to your Highness that this person has no voice in the council.
Boom. Certainly not!
Puck. Only a commanding officer—
Prince P. And a nobleman—
Boom. He's no voice!
Puck. Positively none!
Grand D. Silence, gentlemen! As I'm an honest woman, the first man who speaks without my leave, off goes his head. You said, I think, that to have a voice in the council he should be a commanding officer. I make him a general (*to* Boom) as you are. He ought to be noble—I create him Baron Vermuth von-Boch-Bier, Count Thschalkscoren Vergiss-Mein-Nicht! Is there any other requisite, gentlemen, to entitle him to a voice in the council?
Boom. Your Highness—
Prince P. (*Aside to* Puck.) I say, I say, this wont do, this won't do!
Puck. (*Aside.*) Hush! We'll talk anon.
Grand D. General, take a seat, and let us hear what you have to say.
Fritz. Instead of marching on the enemy by three routes—
Grand D. This collar is just a trifle too high; it wants a good quarter of an inch off to free the neck. There, go on, my friend, don't let me interrupt you. (*Aside.*) What a handsome fellow it is!
Fritz. I was saying that the right way was to march straight upon the enemy; one route will do, and then, when we've got at him, me and the other lads—bang away with all our might—keep banging, banging away, and the business is settled.
Grand D. Excellent! General Boom, that is the plan upon which you'll conduct the campaign.
Boom. I shall do nothing of the kind!
Grand D. How?
Boom. I am responsible to your Highness for the blood sp'lt by your so'diers. Follow my plan—it's a safe thing—no engagement is possible; follow his, and I can answer for nothing.

Grand D. Then you dec'ine?
Boom. I decline; let your friend, the Baron there—I forget how your Highness styled him—
Fritz. Baron von Bermuth-Boch Bier Count Tschalkscoren Vergeiss-Mein-Nicht. (*To the* Grand D.) He hear t well enough—that's all his game—that is!
Boom. Let the Baron carry out his own plan if he pleases.
Fritz. By all means, I'm quite ready.
Grand D. What—and you'll win the battle?
Fritz. Either that or lose it—same as any other man.
Grand D. Baron von Vermuth-Boch-Bier.
Fritz. Your Highness?
Grand D. May the protection of heaved favor your arms. Henceforward you are the Commander-in-Chief of my armies.
Fritz *to* Boom. By your leave you must please to moult those feathers.
Boom. A thousand furies!
Fritz. Ugh! you're a disgrace to the service.
Boom. Ha!
Puck. Restrain your anger—there are three of us thirsting for vengeance, and vengeance we'll have.
Grand D. Upon my honor, he looks splendid, positively splendid. General Fritz, I will forthwith present you to the army as their new Commander-in-Chief. General Boom, order the entire strength of my army under arms.
Boom. I submit to orders!
Puck. Obey,—her heart is touched—my fears are realized.

FINALE.

CHORUS.

On the field of strife soon you'll find us
 Where cannons roar;
Just coasting one fond look behind us
 On to the fore!

RECITATIVE.

Grand Duchess.

Pray listen all, while I, your sovereign, address you.
(*Pointing to* Fritz.) Behold your commander-in-chief!

Chorus.

He! our commander-in-chief!

Grand Duchess.

Yes, my men, and with this I'd impress you,
 He'll come out strong—that's my belief.

Prince Paul, Boom *and* Puck.

All three for dear vengeance uniting
 No risk we'll run,
Jolly odds in our favor fighting,
 We're three to one.

Wanda (*to* Fritz).

A commander-in-chief!

Fritz.

Just so, as you observe.

Wanda.

Poor me you'll quite forget.

Fritz.

From my troth I'll ne'er swerve.

Wanda.

Say will you love me still?

Fritz.

Yes indeed, love I will.

Wanda.

Oh! those dear words repeat.

Fritz.

As often as you will.

Grand Duchess *to* Fritz *and* Wanda *impatiently.*

When you have quite done that private *tete-a-tete*,
It may strike you, perhaps, that your pleasure I wait.

Chorus. *Sotto voce.*

See! she eyes them askance,
With wild rage in her glance.

Grand Duchess.

Why, at their sight, all this emotion?
  Why beats my heart beyond restraint?
Seeing that girl, what secret notion
  All in a flutter sets my nerves. Oh, I s' all faint.
But as a Queen whate'er I feel,
    My dignity maintaining,
    All impulse weak restraining,
All signs of emotion I now must conceal.

(*To* Nepomuc.)

Away and bring me on the spot
That same thing whereof you wot.

(*Enter* Nepomuc.)

All.

What can be her meaning?

(*Enter* Nepomuc.)

All.

The sabre!

Grand Duchess.

Lo, here the sabre of my sire!
  Take thou and hang it at thy side.
High does thy valiant soul aspire.
  Well may this sword become thy pride!
Erst when to battle Pa was starting.
  If his own words may be believed,
From my dear mother, ere departing,
  This dreadful weapon he received.
Lo, here the sabre of my sire!
  Take thou and hang it at thy side.

Chorus.

Lo, here the sabre of her sire !
    Take thou and hang it at thy side.

Grand Duchess *takes the sword*.

Lo, here the sabre of my sire !
    Take thou and hang it at thy side.
Thy star I fear not, trusting rather
    Thee well and hearty home 'twill guide ;
For in the battle shouldst thou perish,
    I very much begin to doubt
If I——by all that most I cherish,
    I had well nigh let something out !

Lo, here the sabre of my sire !
    Take thou and hang it at thy side.

Chorus.

Lo, here the sabre of her sire !
    Take thou and hang it at thy side.

Fritz.

To my hands you may trust, fearless what may befall,
The sabre so revered of your late lamented father,
A victor I'll return, or not return at all !

Grand Duchess.

A victor you'll return.

Boom, Puck, *and* Prince Paul.

He'll not return at all.

Chorus.

He'll return.

Boom, Puck, *and* Prince Paul.

Not at all !

FRANTIC CHORUS.

Fritz.	Boom, Puck, *and* Prince Paul.
Victor I'll come back,	He will ne'er come back,
Pluck since I don't lack,	All his troops they'll hack.
My artiller-y,	His artiller-y,
And my cavalry,	And his cavalry,
And my infantry—	And his infantry,
No fellows can stand	Their jackets they'll dust,
'Gainst such a brave band—	Their boilers they ll bu'st;
Soon we'll send the foe	He'll be by his foe
All to Jericho.	Sent to Jericho.
Their plans we'll forestall,	His plans they'll forestall,
Their troops we'll appal,	His troops they'll appal,
On their backs we'll fall,	On his back they'll fall,
Back their troops they'll call,	Back his troops he'll call,
We'll pursue them all,	They'll pursue them all,
Cut them up quite small,	Cut them up quite small,
Till we've reached their soil.	Till they've reached our soil,
We will forward spring,	They will forward spring,
Then plunder and despoil,	Then plunder and despoil,
Spare no mortal thing.	Spare no mortal thing.

THE OTHERS.

Victor he'll come back
Pluck since he don't lack,
His artilleree,
And his cavalree,
And his infantree
No fellow can stand
'Gainst such a brave band;
Soon he'll send the foe
All to Jericho,
Their plans he'll forestall,
Their troops he'll appal,
On their backs he'll fall,
Back their troops they'll call,
He'll pursue them all,
Cut them up quite small,
Till he's reached their soil,
Forward he will spring.
Then plunder and despoil
Spare no mortal thing.

GRAND CHORUS.

Play up a lively measure,
March away, tra, la, la;
As on a trip of pleasure
Singing heigh! tra, la, la,
Away, away, march away!

THE GRAND DUCHESS. Stay, you forget—the sabre of my sire!

CHORUS.

You had forgot the falchion of her father!

ACT II.

SCENE.—*An apartment in the palace.*

SCENE I.—IZA, CHARLOTTE, AMELIE, OLGA, *and other maids of honor.*

CHORUS OF MAIDS OF HONOR.

The cruel war at last is o'er,
And ended quite is their campaign;
Each lass will now behold once more,
Ere night appear, her faithful swain.

IZA.

Here's the post, run, ladies, quick to meet him,
And for his pains with welcome greet him.

NEPOMUC. Who wants a letter? Quickly say.
ALL. Come this way, good Sir, come this way.
[NEPOMUC, *distributing the letters.*

NEPO. Quickly say.
ALL. Take them, pray.

NEPO.

To yield me passage, lift all latches.
Make way for the Grand Duchess's private despatches.

22

CHARLOTTE, IZA, AMELIE, OLGA.

ENSEMBLE.

Ere rent thy seal how beats each heart?
Missive dear penned by a fond lover;
What fond delight to steal a part,
And con each dear word of thee over.

OLGA.

"I placed o'er my heart the portrait you gave me
When we parted, duck;
From many a wound I knew it would save me,
Just in that place stuck.
Without e'en a scratch if back soon you'll have me,
'Twas that brought me luck."

Ah! letter I treasure;
All day with what pleasure
I'll read thee, nor miss
Each sentence to kiss!

AMELIE.

"It seems we shall cut short this war and bother,
So you'll see me back;
And time being short, and one thing and t'other,
This is now my tack—
Directly I'm home I'll, seeking your mother,
Pop the question smack."

Ah! letter I treasure;
All day with what pleasure
I'll read thee, nor miss
Each sentence to kiss!

CHARLOTTE.

"I did not much like when the fighting began, dear;
At facing the fire I felt in a stew.
However I fought, I fought like a man, dear,
My courage came back when I thought of you."

IZA.

"We yesterday gave the foe a good dressing,
At least I opine;
But what's that to me? there's naught worth possessing
In the conquering line
Save that which I prize above every blessing—
One sweet kiss of thine."

ALL.

Ah! letter I treasure;
All day with what pleasure
I'll read thee, nor miss
Each sentence to kiss!

IZA (*to* OLGA). What is in your letter?
OLGA. All sorts of things. And in yours?
AMELIE (*to* CHARLOTTE). Oh! If you only knew?
CHARLOTTE. Show me!
AMELIE. With all my heart, but you must show yours.
CHARLOTTE. That I will.
OLGA. Oh! that's the way he writes to you, is it?
IZA. Yes; and doesn't yours?
OLGA. So does mine. There—look—the part that is underlined.

[*Enter* PRINCE PAUL *and* BARON GROG.]

PRINCE P. Very well, then, it's quite safe now. Good day, ladies.
A LIE. Good day, Prince Paul.
ME LOTTE. Poor Prince!
IZA. Unfortunate Prince!
PRINCE P. (*to* GROG.) They are poking fun at me.
GROG. I perceive they are.
PRINCE P. I'm not angry with them. Ladies, I have the honor to present to you Baron Grog, the envoy of Papa.
LADIES. Baron!
GROG. Ladies!
PRINCE P. I have a letter of audience for to-day.
IZA. For to-day?
PRINCE P. Yes, for to-day. Will you do the favor to announce to Her Highness that Baron Grog is arrived?
OLGA. But, your Highness, that does not concern us.
CHARLOTTE. You must address yourself to an aide-de-camp.
AMELIE. And here is one.

[*Enter* NEPOMUC.]

NEPO. Grand news, grand news—General Fritz is to have a public reception in the presence of the full court. He returns covered with victory, and her Highness is so delighted—so very delighted.
AMELIE. There is one!
ISA. They're coming back—we shall see them again.

[*Enter* BOOM *and* PUCK.]

PUCK. Go quick, ladies, make haste; the Grand Duchess waits for you.
BOOM. Hasten, ladies.

CHORUS OF MAIDS OF HONOR.

Ah! letter I treasure;
All day with what pleasure
I'll read thee, nor miss
Each sentence to kiss?

PRINCE P. Well, and how about my Grog?
PUCK. Make your mind easy, Prince—your Grog will be served up presantly.
GROG. What!
BOOM. His excellency means that an audience will be granted to the Baron. Usher, introduce his Excellency, Baron Grog, to the presence of Her Highness, and obey the instructions you have received, Baron.
GROG. General, your most obedient.
PRINCE P. Now's the time, Grog, be very impassioned and very insinuating, in fact, be hot, strong and sweet, Grog.

[*Exit* BARON GROG.)

PRINCE P. At last! gentlemen, at last!
PUCK. Come, come, Prince.
PRINCE P. Oh, my dear Baron, you don't know how overcome I am with emotion. She has consented to receive my Grog, he is now on his way to the presence chamber. I see him—there—don't you see him?
BOOM. Certainly.
PRINCE P. He is passing through the first ante-chamber.
PUCK. Right.
PRINCE P. He turns to the left. The hangings are drawn aside, he is in the presence.
BOOM. My dear Prince, you are going a great deal too fast, the Baron has not turned to the left, but to the right, and still preceded by the Usher, and he has come to the bottom of a flight of stairs, which by this time he must be ascending. Conducted through a suite of about twelve apartments to another flight of stairs which he will descend, he will traverse another suite of twelve apartments, re-ascend another flight of stairs, re-descend—
PUCK. Re-ascend?
PRINCE P. And re-redescend.

Puck. And so on, up and down, until he reaches a little door which will be thrown wide open, discovering the Baron's carriage. The Usher will politely invite him to enter it, and inform him that the audience is deferred to another day.

Prince P. And that's to be the order of proceeding?

Boom. Precisely.

Prince P. And the Grand Duchess has had the audacity—

Puck. She has. But really, Prince, you must be out of your senses. With all due respect, positively out of your senses to imagine that on the very day General Fritz returns, and returns crowned with victory, the Grand Duchess can entertain any other thought than that of Fritzing her hair to receive him.

Prince P. Fritz again! curse that fellow!

Boom. He will be here presently and his triumph is assured.

Prince P. Well, it may, it may—but let him wait.

Boom }
Puck } For what?

Prince P. Nothing—nothing—gentlemen, I said nothing—I meant nothing.

Puck. It doesn't take—

Boom. We must tell him all. The enemy! on to the enemy.

Puck. No, no, it's not the enemy, it's *our* enemy.

Prince P. General Fritz has arrived.

Boom. Pardon me, gentlemen, but my sword has been idle for a whole fortnight, and my soul yearns for the fray!

The entire Court enter, preceded by two Ushers.

Grand Chorus.

Our brave troops behold
   Returning glorious from the fray,
On these heroes bold
   Let beauty smile this joyful day.

Grand Duchess.

Now to see him once more! with suspense how I tremble,
Ah! when I meet his gaze can I my love dissemble?

Chorus.

Our brave troops behold, &c.

Fritz.

Four days, madame, suffic'd your enemies to lather.
   Your troops have won the day, the adversary's fled.
Here safe I return to you, as I said,
   The falchion so rever'd of your lamented father.

Grand Duchess.

Lo, here, the falchion of my father.

All.

Lo, here, the falchion of her father.

Grand Duchess.

Let it be placed a glass-case under
In my museum.

To Fritz.   And thou, soldier, tired of war's alarms,
   Before my court, aghast with wonder,
Recite the doughty deeds and exploits of your arms.

Chorus.

Recite the doughty deeds and exploits of your arms,

FRITZ.

Well! you shall learn, your Royal Highness,
    How came about
    This awful route,
And how I, by my skill and slyness,
    The foe surpris'd
    His troop capsiz'd.

RONDO.

All in good order, colors flying,
    Our troops marched forth upon this raid.
Four days elaps'd before espying
    The foe in numbers strong array'd.
At once I made my army halt;
    My plan was laid,
    I'm not afraid
That with it you'll find any fault—
    Without pretence
    One may have sense—
With some score thousand flasks supplied,
    Half of wine, half strong liquor,
What did I? Your ears open wide!
I let the foe the whole secure,
What shouts soon through their camp resound!
    "Ho! there, more wine!
    Your health—here's mine!"
In rosy floods all sense is drown'd;
    Though I said nought
    The more I thought
Next day with hope our spirit buoyed—
    Our challenge they accept to fight.
I saw them all in line deployed,
    But oh! good lord, in what a plight!
All o'er the field you saw them straying,
    Staggering, slipping,
    Tumbling, tripping,
Like a vast field of barley swaying,
    Always inclin'd
    As blows the wind.
Heading this host of jolly topers,
    Their noble chief, flame in his eyes,
Caper'd more drunken than his troopers.
    "What, oh! my buck," to me he cries,
I answered pat, "Come on, old lady!"
    Then like a shot
    The poor old sot,
At each step getting more unsteady,
    Across the field
    Fierce onward reel'd!
You would have held your sides with laughing
    To see this hero in his cups,
Leading an army, laughing, chaffing,
    Sadly in want of "pick me ups."
Ah! ne'er was battle half such fun!
    If you made fall
    One, down came all.
As for the slain, there wasn't one.
    Fate was too kind,
    But never mind.
Bravely your troops, the whole sum tottle,
    Got through this most severe of tasks,
Sleeping on this fam'd field of *bottle*,
    Where the dead men were empty flasks.

ALL. Long live General Fritz.

GRAND D. General, receive my compliments, you speak as eloquently as you fight bravely. *(To the Court.)* Nobles and ladies, this imposing ceremony being now concluded, and the weighty interests of the State requiring that I should impart to General

Fritz certain matters which none but himself may hear, you have our permission to retire. Begone.

PRINCE P. (*To Puck.*) Alone *tête-a-tête* with him.
BOOM. How she's going a-head!
PUCK. (*In a suppressed tone.*) And will you put up with this, P.ince?
PRINCE P. If I could see my way to—
BOOM. Perhaps there is a way.
GRAND D. Begone, ladies and gentlemen of the the Court, begone.

CHORUS.—" Our brave troops."

[*The entire Court retires,* PRINCE PAUL, BOOM *and* PUCK *follow.*]

GRAND D. We are alone.
FRITZ. Yes, not a soul but ourselves.
GRAND D. General.
FRITZ. Your Highness.
GRAND D. I am delighted to see you.
FRITZ. Same here.
GRAND D. Thank you.
FRITZ. Don't mention it pray, don't mention it.
GRAND D. I applaud myself for what I have done. When my glance first rested on you, your position was that of a private soldier.
FRITZ. An obscure private
GRAND D. I raised you to the rank of Commander-in-Chief, and you have beaten the enemy.
FRITZ. We'll ecosh!
GRAND D. Shall we talk of the rewards to which your services entitle you?
FRITZ. I've no objection, but what's the use?
GRAND D. How so?
FRITZ. Look here, let's talk to the point. Arn't I Commander-in-Chief? Very well, then how can I be promoted? I can't go any higher.
GRAND D. That's your idea, is it?
FRITZ. Don't it stand to reason? I've got the plume. I can't go any higher.
GRAND D. In the military department perhaps not, but—
FRITZ. Well?
GRAND D. In the grades of civil employment—
FRITZ. Oh!—Ah (*aside.*) I'm hanged if I'm not grounded now. Never mind; it's something to reward me, so its all right.
GRAND D. A suite of apartments will be prepared for you in the palace. That was decided on this morning at the suggestion of General Boom.
FRITZ. General Boom suggested that?
GRAND D. It was an idea that came to him at my command.
FRITZ. How he must have fumed.
GRAND D. Should you like him sent into exile?
FRITZ. I—not in the least! There's no harm in him at bottom. As for our little tiffs, it all comes of the girls—it's all the girls.
GRAND D. The girls?
FRITZ. Nothing else.
GRAND D. Ah! I suppose you got on pretty well—
FRITZ. Tolerably, thank you, and yourself—
GRAND D. You don't understand me; I mean with the girls—
FRITZ. You mean with the—
GRAND D. Nothing, nothing; never mind—
FRITZ. Oh! very well.
GRAND D. How fortunate is the lowly rustic girl. When a lowly rustic girl loves a lowly rustic youth, she goes straight up to him and says—
FRITZ. Thee's taken my fancy lad.
GRAND D. Accompanying her speech with a moderate nudge of her elbow. But in our sphere it's quite different. We must beat about the bush, drop distant hints. For ins-ance, now there is a lady of my Court who is passionately enamored of you.
FRITZ. A lady of the Court! You're joking.
GRAND D. Well, instead of going straight up to you—
FRITZ. With a moderate nudge of her elbow—
GRAND D. She confessed her love to me.
FRITZ. To you?

DUO

GRAND DUCHESS.

Yes, gallant sir, a heart you've ensnared
At court, the lady well is known,
Herself to state this, unprepared,
She has entreated me her passion deep to own.

FRITZ.

What! Ask'd you?—despite your high station?
Towards you this lady then, no doubt,
Stands in most intimate relation,
For otherwise I can't at all the circumstances make out.

GRAND DUCHESS.

For her well-being I dearly care.

FRITZ.

Such condescension's rare;
I thank you for my share.

GRAND DUCHESS.

Yes, I love her most sincerely.

FRITZ.

Well, this friend you love so dearly,
What said she now
Of me? Pray let me know, I long to hear; I vow—

GRAND DUCHESS.

Thus said the friend I love so blindly:
"Whene'er your eyes throw
On him, kindly
Say to him what so well you know."

RONDO.

Say to him an impress he's made—
Ne'er to fade.
Say to him he's thought most enchanting.
Say to him he has but to pray,
None can say
What in reason one wouldn't be granting,
And rosy wreaths had he a mind
To mingle with his laurels glorious
In conquests of a gentler kind;
This victor still might prove victorious.
Say to him, he e'en at first sight
Charm'd me quite.
Say to him, my wits he's upsetting,
Say to him, I think of him so,
Cruel foe!
Oh! so much—idiotic I'm getting,
Alas my fate, one moment seal'd,
One glance, and no power could restore thee.
My heart I could not help but yield,
I felt that its Lord stood before me,
Say to him, unless he would make
One's heart break,
Say to him, for her mind I am pleading,
Say to him, he'll not answer, nay,
Tell him, pray,

She who loves him hath beauty exceeding!

GRAND DUCHESS.

Now say, what answer make you, pray?

FRITZ.

I must mind what I say,
And prove no fool to-day!

GRAND DUCHESS.

Reply not long, sure, need it take you,
To this lady what answer make you!

FRITZ.

Say to her that my heart is tender.

GRAND DUCHESS.

Every word I'll say.

FRITZ.

For her words my thanks I send her.

GRAND DUCHESS.

Every word I'll say.

FRITZ.

That with ardor my heart is burning.

GRAND DUCHESS.

Every word I'll say.

FRITZ.

Her politeness to be returning.

GRAND DUCHESS.

Every word I'll say.

FRITZ.

All this I say; but e'en though death await me,
If ought I can twig,
Dash my wig, dash my wig;
And may Old Nick this moment spificate me
If I knew who can be this lady.

GRAND DUCHESS.

Speak, pray!

FRITZ

Well, say—Well, say—
Say to her that my heart is tender.

GRAND DUCHESS.

Every word I'll say.

&c.   &c.

ENSEMBLE.

GRAND DUCHESS.

My meaning at once he has caught,
For the heart oft quickens the thought.

FRITZ.

Of this I understand just nought,
Though a fool never yet was I thought.

FRITZ. Hum! All these honors and titles I now possess, including my plume; if I want to keep them—and I do—this lady of the Court and friend of the Grand Duchess—I cannot do better than—
GRAND D. General?
FRITZ. But then there's Wanda—dear little Wanda—confoundedly bothering!
GRAND D. General?
FRITZ. Your Highness.
GRAND DUCHESS. Come nearer to me.
FRITZ. It's confoundedly bothering.
GRAND D. No—no—be se ted—there. How well those orders become you. If there are any others you would like to have, you have only to ask—but I am wandering. What was I saying? Oh, that lady I was speaking about; you haven't given me any answer yet; you confined yourself to general expressions—
FRITZ. Well, ecosh! seeing that I'm a general.
GRAND D. Capital! capital! But a truce to pleasantry. You really must answer.
FRITZ. So, then, the lady in question not only asked you to deliver her message, but to bring back the answer as well?
GRAND D. Exactly so. Well?
FRITZ. Ah!
GRAND D. What's the matter?
FRITZ. Nothing, only in arranging my collar you slightly—
GRAND D. Oh! I beg your pardon.
FRITZ. Granted.
GRAND D. But come! your answer. Say you were by that lady's side as now you are at mine, what would you say to her?
FRITZ. Well, ecosh?
GRAND D. That's pretty well, so far, only it's an expression you use rather frequently; but you say it so well. Come, proceed. After saying well, ecosh!
FRITZ. To tell you the truth, I should be confoundedly puzzled.

(Enter NEPOMUC.)

NEPO. Your Highness.
GRAND D. Who's there? Did I call?
NEP. The chief of your secret police awaits an audience, your Highness.
GRAND D. Oh! I haven't time at this moment.
NEP. Pardon me, your Highness; the matter he has to communicate is of the deepest importance.
GRAND D. Give it me.
FRITZ. *(Aside.)* Ah! if it wasn't for little Wanda—dear little Wanda—its confoundedly bothering.
GRAND D. "Public Scandal—indecorous behaviour of General Fritz—the young girl Wanda brought by him into the capital.' Oh! this is too outrageous. *(To NEPOMUC.)*—You said the chief of my police was waiting?
NEP. Yes, your Highness.
GRAND D. *(Aside.)* Wanda! impossible! *(To FRITZ.)* General, in an instant I will be with you again—will you excuse me?
FRITZ. Oh, yes, I'll excuse you.
GRAND D. Wait for my return. *(To NEPOMUC.)* Captain Nepomuc, attend me.
[*Exit followed by NEPOMUC.*]

FRITZ. Well, now, here's a pretty situation! If I say to this lady, "I am very sorry I can't love you, being previously engaged," she'll be furious. Very ridiculous of her, but she will. Why isn't it quite common when you're invited to dinner, for instance, to answer "Very sorry a prior engagement." Of course that doesn't mean you turn up your nose at the dinner, but simply that you have had an earlier invitation. Consequently, if the lady loses her temper she'll be in the wrong. I'll go at once and tell the Duchess I've a previous invitation, she'll tell the lady, and it'll be all right.

Enter PAUL, BOOM *and* PUCK.

FRITZ. Ah! Ah! there come my three amiable friends.
PUCK. He's here.
BOOM. Won't he be confoundedly in the way if we are to have our talk!
NEPOMUC (*to* FRITZ.) General!
FRITZ. What is it, Captain?
NEPOMUC. Business of State detains her Highness, who has commanded me conduct you to your apartments in the right wing of the palace.
PUCK. (*aside to* PAUL.) Do you hear? His apartments in the right wing?
FRITZ (*to* NEPOMUC). Oh! Very well, Captain, (*Aside*). That's it. I'll just tell straight out, that, all things considered, I intend to marry Wanda, and I'll marry off-hand at once. Now, Captain, for the right wing. Gentlemen!—
PRINCE P. ⎫
BOOM. ⎬ General.
PUCK. ⎭
FRITZ. I say, poor young soldier's got on in the world a bit!
BOOM. Did you address me?
FRITZ. Ugh?—disgrace to the service!

(*Exit* FRITZ *followed by* NEPOMUC.)

PUCK. She has commanded apartments to be prepared for him in the right wi You heard, the right wing!
BOOM. It's only what was to be expected.
PUCK. Exactly so. But you don't understand our meaning.
PRINCE P. Not in the least.
PUCK. Ah—well—you shall soon see it all as plain as a pike-staff. Look at t picture.
PRINCE P. Yes, I'm looking at it.
PUCK. Just go and exert a smart pressure against the left boot of that noble p sonage.
PRINCE P. I beg your pardon. What did you say.
BOOM. He says—you're to exert a smart pressure.
PRINCE P. Ah—it's some trick now.
PUCK. No trick, upon my honor.
PRINCE P. I'm sure I know what it is—there's a spring—and something will off, and hit me in the eye.
BOOM. Nothing of the kind—go on—push!
PRINCE P. Hullo a blind beggar with his clarionet—
BOOM. You're mistaken.
PUCK. It is the screech owl's dismal cry. Years have elapsed since yonder do was opened. About two hundred years ago—
PRINCE P. You would seem to have some moving story to relate.
BOOM. A horrible tale!
PRINCE P. Unfold it.
PUCK. I will—to yonder passage there are two extremities—
PRINCE P. Most passages have two extremities on an average.
PUCK. One opens out into this apartment, the other communicates with the rig wing where the General's quarters have been prepared.
PRINCE P. Ah!
PUCK. At this end is the portrait of a man—at the other the portrait of a lady. open the secret panel here you press against the man's boot—at the other end you pr the lady's knee—
PRINCE P. Press her knee?
PUCK. A fanciful idea of the painter's. When amongst the living the individ whose portrait you there behold was called Count Max Winkin von Knockemoff. T portrait at the other end is that of his spouse, the Grand Duchess Victorine, ancestor our present Sovereign.
PRINCE P. Proceed -

BOOM.

A horrible tale—a soul harrowing story.

PUCK.

These ancient walls retain its traces grim and gory.

BOOM.

Count Max conquer'd fortune right early.

Thanks to his sword,
His bright eyes and moustache so cur'y
　　Ladies adored.
The Duchess with discrimination
　　Gave him her heart,
And the right wing for his habitation
　　She set apart.
Each night love with due caution wedding
　　Max at that door,
Would list for a light footstep threading
　　Yon corridor.

　　PRINCE PAUL, BOOM *and* PUCK.

List to this horrible tale,
List, oh list, and the sad lot bewail,
Which untimely cut off
Brave young Count Max von Winkin Knockemoff.

　　PUCK.

One night Max with senses confounded
　　Marked in affright
That the step of his fair lady sounded
　　Not quite so light.
This gave him a sort of a shake up.
　　He saw his fate
Too late for a bolt his mind to make up.
　　That step of weight
Announced some dozen brisk young fellows
　　Resolved quite
To make a hole in Max's bellows
　　Ere morning's light.

　　PAUL.

Twelve men of blood—

　　BOOM.

　　　　Closely masked o'er.

　　ALL.

Came through yon door!

　　ENSEMBLE.

&c.　　　&c.　　　&c.

Now the Prince surely understands.

　　PAUL.

I understand—see my emotion.

　　BOOM.

This Fritz must perish by our hands.

　　PAUL.

You don't say so—what an odd notion.

　　PUCK *and* BOOM.

Yes, he must perish by our hands.

BOOM.

We'll quarter him this very night,
In that same wing they call the right,
We'll quarter him, the gallant spark,
Safely caged in yon passage dark.

ENSEMBLE.

We'll quarter him this very night,
&c. &c.

PAUL.

When of night the solemn hours advance,
  Friend Fritz may, on lawful rights encroaching,
At his door listen if perchance
  He hear not some light step approaching.
    A step so dear
    And light draw near,
    So light so dear
    Draw softly near,
    A pretty step draw softly near.

ALL THREE.

Don't he wish that step he may hear?
Oh dear no—of that there's no fear.

BOOM.

When wild dreams his vision entrancing,
  He exclaims "a Grand Duke—here's luck,"
Lo, sudden through the gloom advancing,
  Behold us three, Paul, Boom and Puck!

PAUL.

Yes, behold, 'tis I—Paul.

BOOM.

And behold, 'tis Boom.

PUCK:

And behold 'tis I—Puck.

ENSEMBLE.

We'll quarter him this very night,
&c. &c.

Enter the GRAND DUCHESS.

PRINCE P. Then it's an understood thing, we form a conspiracy.
BOOM *and* PUCK. We form a conspiracy.
PRINCE P. We will meet an hour hence at my residence, if that will suit you, and draw up a plan of action.
PUCK. Any refreshments?
PRINCE P. Necessarily.
BOOM. Any ladies?
PRINCE P. What, women in a conspiracy! Boom, Boom! What can you be thinking of?
GRAND D. By your leave, gentlemen, there will be one lady in your conspiracy.
ALL THREE. Her Highness!
GRAND D. Her Highness.
PUCK. We're lost.
PRINCE P. Nothing left but to make a bolt of it.

GRAND D. Gentlemen, you have nothing to fear. You are conspiring against General Fritz. Enrol me among your number.
BOOM. Can your Highness mean it?
PUCK. (*Aside.*) That's how the land lies, eh?
PRINCE P. (*Aside.*) After all, it's better so for all parties.
GRAND D. Are you aware of General Fritz's latest proceedings? He has sent to me requesting my consent to his marriage with Wanda. That consent I have granted. The General is now before the altar of the Chapel in the Palace, and from thence he will proceed to—
ALL THREE. Proceed where?
GRAND D. To the spot—where you will lie in wait for him—his apartment in the right wing.
ALL THREE. The right wing!

ENSEMBLE.

We'll quarter him this very night, &c.

ACT III.

TABLEAU THE FIRST.

SCENE I.—*The Crimson Chamber.*

GRAND DUCHESS *then* BOOM.

BOOM. Your Highness!
GRAND D. Well, General, where did you leave him?
BOOM. At his own wedding ball—dancing. He was executing with extraordinary agility the step called *cavalier seul*.
GRAND D. Dancing! and in a brief space that man, now so full of life and vigor, will be a—but are all your precautions taken for the deed were he to make his appearance now?
BOOM. No fear of that. I informed him it was your Highness's express command, he was not to leave the ball till the last country dance was over.
GRAND D. And how did he receive that command?
BOOM. With every sign of dissatisfaction. He exclaimed "That's a treat when a man's just starting on his wedding trip."
GRAND D. He said that, did he?
BOOM. Those very words.
GRAND D. How he doats on that little chit of a thing, but patience, patience!
BOOM. What is your Highness gazing at?
GRAND D. Look there upon those boards, a broad dark deep stain, 'tis blood! to visitors who come to view the interior of the Palace, that stain is pointed out. "On that spot," they are told, "Count Max fell assassinated." Whether it is so or not I'm sure I dont know, but the porter at the palace gate says so, and he makes a tidy thing by it.
BOOM. Dating from to morrow two stains will darken that floor, and two little incomes will accrue to the porters of the palace.
GRAND D. In all probability—but where are your accomplices?
BOOM. They await my signal, stationed in yonder secret passage.

GRAND D. Open the door, and let them enter, while I conceal myself behind the arras.

BOOM. That'll be capital.

GRAND D. Why will that be capital?

BOOM Because if your Highness were not concealed there the plot would be deficient in the feminine element.

GRAND D. Ah, good! but take care you don't reveal my presence. In due time, and when I think proper, I shall show myself.

BOOM. Your Highness.

GRAND D. Now, summon your friends, and oblige me by carrying this business through smartly.

BOOM. (*Alone.*) There's the portrait; now for the secret spring. (*Enter* PUCK, PRINCE PAUL NEPOMUC, *and* BARON GROG.) One, two, three, four—where are the rest?

PUCK. They will be at hand at the proper time. If we had all come together such simultaneous rush might have excited suspicion.

BOOM. Quite right!

PRINCE P. First of all, we must settle exactly what we're to do.

BOOM. (*To* NEPOMUC.) Captain, are you in our little affair?

NEPOMUC. Well, General, when I found it was agreeable to the Grand Duchess feelings—

PRINCE P. Sly dog!

NEPO. I am a poor man, sir, but I desire to better myself.

BOOM. Give me your hand, Captain.

NEPO. There is my hand, General.

BOOM. I esteem a man of your stamp. (*To* PRINCE PAUL). Does the Baron join us Prince?

PRINCE P. Yes, General.

ALL. Baron.

GROG. Gentlemen.

PUCK. The Baron is acquainted with the nature of this business.

GROG. Oh, perfectly. Somebody's to be killed.

PRINCE P. It's to be done in this apartment.

PUCK. Yes, here, here the blow is to be struck.

BOOM. And now I have a word to say to all present.

PUCK. What are you going to do now?

PRINCE P. Pray, put that up.

ALL. Put it up, put it up.

BOOM. When a man engages in a business of this kind, he must carry it through without flinching. The first man who shows any disposition to flinch I'll slice him into four quarters.

PRINCE P. Pray put up your sword.

PUCK. Haven't you been told nobody wants to flinch?

BOOM. What I've said I've said.

PRINCE P. There now, drop the subject.

Enter the GRAND DUCHESS.

GRAND D. Gentlemen, are you quite sure your daggers are of true steel?

THE CONSPIRATORS. Your Highness.

GRAND D. Concealed yonder I have been the unseen witness of all, resolving to present myself at the last moment in order, if requisite, to urge on your resolution; but am glad to perceive you need it not.

NEPO. I rather think not.

PUCK. Let him come, and you shall see.

BOOM. I'll slice him into four quarters.

GRAND D. Gentlemen, there is one request I have to make.

PUCK. Say a command, your Highness.

GRAND D. Let me impress upon you, above all things, not to disfigure his countenance—spare his countenance.

GROG. Such a pity to spoil his handsome countenance.

GRAND D. Who said that?

GROG. I did.

GRAND D. Who are you? I know every one of the conspirators who are here, but you I never saw before.

PRINCE P. That's my Grog.

GRAND D. Your Grog?

PRINCE P. Don't you know? Baron Grog—papa's envoy, whom you refused to grant an audience to.

GRAND D. I have been much in fault for so doing.

Boom. Your Highness!
Grand D. Nothing, nothing Go and post your men, gentlemen, and when you have done so, return all three; you, Baron Grog, I wish to remain.
Grog. Your Highness!
Grand D. Well, what? Have you not requested that I would grant you an audience? Very well; that audience I am now about to grant you. Begone, gentlemen, begone.
Prince P. I'll just give my Grog a slight stir up. Grog, be hot and strong, Grog.
Grand D. The first thing that struck me about you, Baron, is that you look such a good creature.
Grog. Your Highness!
Grand D. What I call a thoroughly good creature.
Grog. It is your pleasure, then, I presume, that we should converse on the subject of my master, the Prince?
Grand D. Yes, but that'll do presently. Allow me, first of all, to express how gratified I am that I can call a person like yourself by the name of friend.
Grog. I beg your pardon.
Grand D. Am I not right—or surely you would not be among those who are about to avenge me?
Grog. As regards that part of the matter, I confess I am not precisely actuated by friendship. Your Highness obstinately refused to receive me; consequently I was left with nothing to do—got bored, and joined the conspiracy to kill time.
Grand D. Only to kill time?
Grog. That's all.
Grand D. How I do admire your style of conversation. You come out with things enough to blow one up in the air, and not a muscle of your face moves.
Grog. The result of education.
Grand D. Indeed!
Grog. From my earliest childhood my relatives destined me to the diplomatic career; so I was taught to preserve an impassive countenance—when I was quite a little chin.
Grand D. Some time ago though.
Grog. Yes, a considerable time ago. When I was quite a little fellow, whenever I was caught not having an impassive countenance I got knocked about.
Grand D. Poor, dear little fellow. Will you allow me to give you just one word of advice?
Grog. With the greatest pleasure.
Grand D. By-and-by, when the time has come to pitch into General Fritz, don't you put yourself forward—you might get a slash across the face, and be disfigured for life.
Grog. That's true.
Grand D. Keep behind the others, and when the affair is over and the time has come to recompense the actors, I shall put you before the others. What's the matter? Just now your lips gave a twitch—so—. If it had been any one else I shouldn't have noticed, but with you it must be equivalent to a violent explosion of laughter.
Grog. Quite correct.
Grand D. Haven't I reckoned you up already? Well, what is it makes you laugh so uncontrollably, tell me?
Grog. Can't
Grand D. Not my friend, then?
Grog. Yes, I am.
Grand D. Then why don't you act as such?
Grog. An hour ago you expressed fears for the safety of General Fritz's countenance, you now express fears for that of mine.
Grand D. By Jove, that's true.
Grog. Putting this and that together, if a fellow was at all conceited he might draw inferences.
Grand D. Musn't do that.
Grog. Oh! no.
Grand D. We won't go on with that subject.
Grog. Suppose we return to my master, the Prince.
Grand D. That'll do presently. What's your position at your own Court? Chamberlain?
Grog. I also hold the rank of Colonel, but only in the palace.
Grand D. I can offer you better than that, if you feel inclined to leave the Court of the Elector.
Grog. I'm sorry to say that's not possible.
Grand D. Not possible!
Grog. That is, unless your Highness consents to marry the Prince, my master.
Grand D. Tut! tut! tut!

Grog. It would then be a matter of course.
Grand D. Marry the Prince? What, you still will hark back to that subject?
Grog. I had imagined we had never digressed from it.
Grand D. Baron, my compliments—you are a wonderful diplomatist.
Grog. Let me entreat your Highness to accept the Prince, he is really a very ni[ce] young man.
Grand D. A wonderful diplomatist, there's no gainsaying.
Grog. Well, your Highness, I await your decision.
Grand D. If you must be answered, Baron, I really can't tell you anything at [all] about it.
Grog. How?
Grand D. The fact is, my head is all in a whirl. All my ideas go whirling, whi[rl]ing, whirling. Fritz, you, Prince Paul and Puck and Boom in the background. Sh[all] he be killed or shall he not? And if any one's killed, who shall it be? Shall it be Fr[itz] —shall it be you?
Grog. Me!
Grand D. Well, I can't tell; and that's what it has come to—I really can't tell y[ou] anything at all about it.

Enter Paul, Boom *and* Puck.

All Three. Your Highness!
Grand D. What is it—what is the matter? Oh, it's you!
Prince P. Well?
Grog. All right.
Prince P. Oh, oh—my dearest friend!
Grand D. Have you posted your men?
Boom. We have.
Grand D. Good. Now go back and tell them they may all go home to their fam[i]lies.
Puck. Eh?
Grand D. There's to be no killing.
Boom. No killing! That's beyond a joke.
Grand D. I beg pardon. What did you say?
Boom. Nothing. I say nothing because your Highness is present; if your Highne[ss] were not present I should say the thing is not to be borne.
Grand D. General, it seems to me you forget yourself.
Boom. No, I don't mean—but look here—wasn't everything all settled? and no[w] just at the last moment—
Prince P. It is really very annoying—after taking no end of trouble.
Puck. All the trouble was over, and nothing left but the pleasure.
Grand D. I have said it—there's to be no killing.
Boom. But why not?
Grand D. What? kill a man on the day of my betrothal? It would be highly u[n]becoming.
Puck. The day of your betrothal?
Prince P. You have said the word, adored one, you have said the word.
Grand D. I have.
Prince P. And you really and positively consent at last.
Grand D. Really and positively I consent; and you may thank the Baron there [for] it. I was overcome by his eloquence.
Prince P. O, Baron, look here! Papa allows me to create a Margrave once a year [and] he prefers that to giving me money—I say no more.
Grand D. Now General—now Baron—what have you to say?
Puck. Your Highness, we admit that on the day you have consented to acquiesce [in] the suit of his Highness, Prince Paul, it would be extremely out of place to—
Boom. Granted; but it's very annoying all the same. That fellow, Fritz, has play[ed] me every kind of scurvy trick; robbed me of my commander-in-chief's plume, depriv[ed] me of the affections of one who might have made me happy, and I'm not to be revenge[d]. (*With explosive energy.*) The enemy! where's the enemy—
Grand D. If that's all, General, you may have your revenge, and welcome. Play hi[m] any trick you like in return, provided you—
Boom. We confine ourselves to the fantastic and humorous.
Grand D. Precisely!
Boom. In that case all right.
Grand D. They are conducting him hither. Find out some good trick to play hi[m]; that's your affair. Prince Paul—
Prince P. Adored one!

GRAND D. In two hours hence I shall await you in the State room for the ceremony of troth plighting. No, Prince, not yet. Gentlemen, Heaven be with you.
PUCK. Here he comes—what shall we do to him? *Exit*.
BOOM. My little scheme is matured—he shall have a wedding trip he little bargained for.

Enter FRITZ and WANDA, escorted by the gentlemen and ladies of the Court.

CHORUS.

Thus far the blushing bride escorting,
We leave her now—our task is done.
In wedlock as in love's disporting,
Two's company, but three is none.
Thus far the blushing bride escorting,
Two's company, but three is none.

FRITZ. Thanks, ladies and gentlemen—thanks for your courteous escort. *(To BOOM, PUCK and GROG.)* You here, gentlemen—
PUCK. Yes, we wished personally to congratulate you and do you honor.
FRITZ. I feel very much flattered, and having done me all the honor in your power, perhaps you'll now do me the pleasure—
PUCK. To go.
FRITZ. Well, ecosh! I think we may say good-night and good-bye.

PUCK (*to* FRITZ.)

Gallant Sir, we bid you good-night!

THE REST.

Good-night.

PUCK.

Those simple words contain a tomb,
If faith adorn not now your home,
You may henceforth to all delight,
Bid good-night.

CHORUS.

Good-night!

BOOM (*to* WANDA.)

And you, fair lady, we bid you good-night.

CHORUS.

Good-night!

If from your side your spouse should roam,
With winning smiles still lure him home;
Grudge not your love or to all delight
Bid good-night.

CHORUS.

Good-night!
[*Exeunt all, except* FRITZ *and* WANDA.]

FRITZ. They're gone at last—thank heaven.
WANDA. I'm not at all sorry.
FRITZ. Nor I, nor I.
WANDA. I mean to say that now they've all done congratulating you it's my turn now to pay you my compliments.
FRITZ. Simple child.
WANDA. Most noble commander-in-chief—

FRITZ. Ah! I say there's a slight difference between being about to marry a simple private, poor and without prospects, and finding yourself the lady of a generalissimo crowned with victorious laurels.

WANDA. Of course, and at first it is a little—

FRITZ. Confess guileless infant, confess that you are dazzled—taken aback.

WANDA. No, not exactly that—but—

FRITZ. Yes you are dazzled—and why! Does my plume strike you with awe, and my laced coat, and my epaulettes, and my orders? Then let me doff the worthless rubbish.

WANDA. What are you about?

FRITZ. Removing your vain terrors.

WANDA. I'm not so sure about that.

FRITZ. Come, come, you really must get familiarized with your position. Why, aren't I your husband? Then why make a bugbear of me?

WANDA. It's true it's very silly of me.

SONG.

I.

Oft *tête-à-tête* we've been together,
How silly then to feel so strange!
Yet that laced coat I wish he'd change,
And take away that horrid feather.
Oft *tête-à-tête* we've been together.
Then surely I've no cause to fear
My husband dear.

WANDA. Heavens! what's that?

FRITZ. Can't say.

("Long live General Fritz!" *Shouts without.*)

WANDA. They're calling you.

FRITZ. It's a serenade, my dear, a most undoubted serenade, in honor of my late victory. The proceeding is flattering, but the moment is awkwardly chosen.

(*Shouts again,* "Long live the General!")

WANDA. How long are they going on so?

FRITZ. Until I address them.

WANDA. Oh, then pray do address them; you must own this sort of thing is anything but pleasant.

FRITZ. Friends, countrymen and drummers, I need not tell you how deeply I feel this attention on your part, at the same time you are, perhaps, not aware that this is my wedding night; consequently, my friends, you perceive—I wish you a very good-night, good-night!

FRITZ. There, that's over, and now, dearest Wanda, no more of this absurd timidity.

II.

We braves may loving be, tho' dreaded,
I'm a great war chief that's confest,
But neath my war-paint heaves a breast
Where martial ire and love are wedded.
Yes, I'm loving dear, tho' dreaded,
Ah, surely you've no cause to fear
Thy husband dear.

WANDA. More serenading!

FRITZ. The military bands—we ought to have been prepared for that—they always strike up after the drums.

WANDA. Now, isn't this too bad?

FRITZ. Wait a bit, I'll address them. Friends, countrymen and musicians! (You perceive the delicate attention—most delicate.)

—My musical friends! I am sorry you did not meet the drummers on your way here—they would have told you that this is my wedding night; consequently, you perceive—I wish you a very good night! good night, my musical friends, good night.

FRITZ. They're off, and won't trouble us again I promise you. And now, dearest Wanda, let us resume our convesation. Let me see, where did I leave off. Ah, yes, I know.

WANDA. What in the world is that, now?

CHORUS (*Outside*).

Open your doors! open them wide!
Ere by main force the bolts we shatter,
Open your doors, bridegroom and bride,
Ere down about your ears they clatter.

WANDA.

Oh, Fritz! don't open, pray.

FRITZ.

All right, dear.

WANDA.

Oh, see the door is yielding! I shall faint, love, with fear.

Enter PRINCE PAUL, PUCK, BOOM, GROG, *and other personages of the court, the* MAIDS OF HONOR *and* PAGES.

PRINCE PAUL, PUCK, BOOM *and* GROG.

Now, kind fortune be praised, we've not arriv'd too late.

FRITZ *and* WANDA.

What heither brings a crowd so great.

PUCK.

Quick to horse!—quick to horse!
And take command of all your force!

CHORUS.

Quick to horse!—quick to horse!
And take command of all your force!

PRINCE PAUL.

Away at once, don't shiliy, shally,
There's not a minute to be lost;
The enemy have made a rally,
And soon our frontiers will have crost.

CHORUS.

Away at once, &c., &c.

BOOM.

Our mistress sends this message, greeting,
About the job don't puff and blow;
Nor think again her eyes of meeting
Until you've routed quite the foe.

CHORUS.

Our mistress sends this, &c., &c.

FRITZ.

But, my friends, are you aware
We have but this instant been made a wedded pair?

BOOM.

To such commands that's no reply,
Away to conquer or to die!

FRITZ.

My wife, in that case, I must leave you.

PUCK.

Very good—sorry to bereave you.
Now haste away,
No more delay.

FRITZ.

My sword-belt now I want to find,
The battle's brunt since I must weather;
M word-belt can't be left behind.

CHORUS.

Behold, 'tis here—it won't be left behind.

FRITZ.

My sabretash—both were together!

CHORUS.

Both were together!

FRITZ.

And now my feather!
Now my feather!
That badge of high command—my plume
Now let me assume.

CHORUS.

He's got his plume.
Stop, dear sir, here's something you forgot—
Behold the thing whereof you wot.

FRITZ.

What, still that falchion!
Oh, did'st thou know—sword of her father—
Than see you, what I wouldn't rather!

CHORUS.

Now haste away
Without delay.

FRITZ.

Who would not be a soldier gay?

CHORUS.

Quick to horse!—quick to horse!
And take command of all your force.
   Quick to horse!
Away at once, don't shilly shally.
Against the foe you forth must sally
   Quick to horse!

SCENE II.—*The Encampment of the First Act.*

CHORUS.

Valiant boys at feast or in battle,
Drink we deep—good liquors rare,
Quaff lads and sing, let your cups rattle,
As we toast the new plighted pair.

BOOM *to* PRINCE PAUL.

So at last, then, her Highness
Deigns your patient hopes to crown.

CHORUS.

To the health of her Highness
Drink a cup of Rhenish down.

PRINCE PAUL.

However I came thus situated,
 Can any fellow understand;
But yesterday next door to hated,
 And now to me she plights her hand.

CHORUS.

Plights her hand!

Enter the GRAND DUCHESS.

GRAND DUCHESS.

I greet you, loyal friends.

PUCK.

Ah, the Duchess.

PRINCE PAUL.

Go seek her,
And hither bring a flowing beaker.

BOOM.

The newly plighted pair drink with loud ringing shout

GRAND DUCHESS.

In that case, dearest friends, I'll join you in a bout

BALLAD.

There liv'd in times, now long gone by,
A Duke among my predecessors,
Whose vaunt it was that he could vie
At drinking with the best professors.

CHORUS.

Whose vaunt it was that he could vie
At drinking with the best professors.

GRAND DUCHESS.

The beaker he was wont to drain
Took twenty full quarts to replenish,
His henchman o'er and o'er again
Unceasing fill'd it high with Rhenish.

CHORUS.

His henchman o'er and o'er again.
Unceasing fill'd it high with Rhenish

GRAND DUCHESS.

Ah, dear old man, how he could swill,
And what a cup was his to fill !

CHORUS.

Ah, good old times, when folks could swill,
And had such monstrous cups to fill.

II.

GRAND DUCHESS.

One day, somehow, it came to pass,
It fell and was to atoms shivered,
And as he sigh'd, "There goes my glass,"
His voice with deep emotion quiver'd

CHORUS.

And, as he sighed, "There goes my glass,"
His voice with deep emotion quiver'd.

GRAND DUCHESS.

Another, when they brought next day,
"No," said he, "that's not my old goblet,
From life I'd rather pass away,
Than from another drink one droplet."

CHORUS.

From life he rather pass'd away,
Than from another drink one droplet.

GRAND DUCHESS.

Ah, dear old man how he would swill
&c. &c.

CHORUS.

Ah, good old times, when folks could swill !

PRINCE P. My dear wife !
GRAND D. Well my husband?
PRINCE P. At last my happiness is assure'd—henceforth I am yours, and you are mine !
GRAND D. Hum ! well perhaps you may venture to say so.
PRINCE P. And this felicity I owe to Baron Grog. We really must find some suitable way of rewarding him.

GRAND D. That's your view?
PRINCE P. That's my view.
GRAND D. Your desires are now my commands. But what can I do for him? All the honors I had at my disposal I have conferred on another. Baron Puck—General Boom—
GEN. BOOM. } Your Highness.
PUCK.
GRAND D. What has become of General Fritz? I was assured by you I should find him in the camp.
PUCK. He cannot fail to be here ere long. In obedience to your highness's instructions, and keeping strictly within the bounds of the fantastic and the ludicrous, we have made him the victim of a slight sell.
GRAND D. May I ask what the sell was?
BOOM. Your Highness, pardon a soldier's bluntness. The case stands thus: For some time past my visits to a certain lady, who shall be nameless in the absence of her lord and master, have excited the jealousy of the latter.
GRAND D. Oh, General, General!
BOOM. My fair friend sent me a small note to this effect: "Don't come to-morrow; he is furious at your persisting to call. He says he'll wait for you, and vows dire vengeance." An idea came to me; I find out General Fritz, and tell him: Proceed at once to Coq à Pic; there you will find the forty-third of the fifty-second and the fifty-second of the forty-third!
GRAND D. And he went—
BOOM. He went; but instead of the forty-third of the fifty-second and the fifty-second of the forty-third, he has by this time encountered the indignant husband.
GROG. Likewise the indignant husband's walking stick.
BOOM. Half-an-hour to go there, and half-an-hour's conversation with the husband, and an hour and a half to limp back to camp, would make him about due now.
BOOM. Timed him to a minute!

Enter WANDA.

Ah! see my good man home returning
From some exploit. With ardor burning,
And on deeds of Prowess bent,
Look how his clothing he has rent.

Enter FRITZ.

I.

FRITZ.

Behold, here your Highness am I—
    Oh my eye!
The mauling I just have come by.
    Oh my eye.
Should count for as good as a fight,
    For ain't I
In a sad and most piteous plight?
Your falchion see, once straight and bright,
Knocked into a cork-screw quite.
    Oh my eye!
Yes, ecoah! he's come to grief,
Your valiant Commander-in-Chief.

CHORUS.

Yes, ecoah! he's come to grief,
Our valiant Commander-in-Chief.

II.

A husband I met on my way—
    Curse the day!
Says he I've got something to say!
    Come here, pray,
I answer in a tone light and gay:
    "Fire away!"
When my back he begins to pay,

     Whack-a-Whack—and a tune there to play
     That will haunt me to my dying day.
     Yes, ecosh! he's come to sad grief,
     Your valiant Commander-in-Chief.

GRAND D. And this is all the explanation you have to offer for your conduct?
FRITZ. All, and quite enough too.
GRAND D. So then, instead of leading my army to the field as I commanded, you have been embroiling yourself in a paltry attempt to disturb the peace of families.
FRITZ. Well, that's a nice way of putting it
GRAND D. Your offence, Sir, is high treason. And is this a plight in which to come into my presence?
FRITZ. Now haven't I told you all about it?
GRAND D. Look at the falchion of my father. What does it look like?
FRITZ. It was that confounded fellow with his cane.
BOOM. Ugh! You disgrace the service.
FRITZ. What's that? Take care what you say.
PUCK. In my humble opinion, your Highness, but one course is before us. A drumhead court-martial on the spot.
FRITZ. A court-martial!
GRAND D. Yes, ecosh!
FRITZ. You can't touch me with a court-martial. As a noble of the realm I can only be tried by my peers.
GRAND D. Indeed, suppose I cancel your patent of nobility. From this moment you cease to be a Count.
FRITZ. You've got me there!
GRAND D. What think you of that, Colonel?
FRITZ. Colonel! I thought I was a General.
GRAND D. I said Colonel.
FRITZ. Oh! very well, suppose you say Captain next.
GRAND D. With all my heart, Captain.
FRITZ. Why not Lieutenant?
GRAND D. Lieutenant, be it so.
FRITZ. That's all right! All right, hadn't you better go on to Sergeant?
GRAND D. Certainly, Sergeant.
FRITZ. Good again, good again.
GRAND D. Why stop, there are more rounds of the ladder yet. Corporal comes next.
FRITZ. And one more sthp down—private Fritz.
GRAND D. Private Fritz you are.
FRITZ. Private Fritz?
GRAND D. Private Fritz.
BOOM. I said I'd be one with you—ugh—you disgrace to the service.
FRITZ. A private, eh? Very well, then, I apply for my discharge.
GRAND D. Granted!
FRITZ. Much obliged; I wish you a very good evening. Come along, Wanda.
GRAND D. Now, then, all these honors and dignities are at my disposal.
BOOM. Ah! a beam of hope dawns upon me.
GRAND D. Prince, I am now in a position to gratify your wishes. Baron Grog, approach.
GROG. Your Highness I obey.
GRAND D. Henceforth the plume of Commander-in-Chief is yours—take it—wear it.
BOOM. Confound him
GRAND D. Wear this also—the sabre of my father.
BOOM. Furies!
GRAND D. Baron Grog, the supreme authority of the State, civil and military, is vested in your hands.
GROG. Your Highness, you have earned the blessings of a devoted wife.
GRAND D. What's that?
GROG. The Baroness Grog will forever bless you
GRAND D. Your Grog possesses a wife?
PRINCE P. A wife and three small children
GROG. Pardon me, four; since our sojourn here I am the proud parent of a fourth.
GRAND D. A wife and four small Grogs—and I had kept him bottled up in reserve, in case at the last moment I should feel inclined to change my mind. Wretched Grog!
GROG. Your Highness.
GRAND D. Give up the plume—give up the falchion—General Boom—resume—the
BOOM. This time I'll have a blacksmith to rivet it on my head.

GRAND D. BARON PUCK—take this—corkscrew—I appoint you custodian of the sabre of my father.
PUCK. I have a duplicate made.
FRITZ. Go it! They have all got sealed patents, but I've got the whacks
GRAND D. Come, I won't be too hard. What post would you like?
FRITZ. A village schoolmaster
GRAND D. Can you read and write?
FRITZ. That's just i —I want to learn
GRAND D. The appointment is granted
FRITZ. And Fritz is thankful
GRAND D. As for you Baron Grog—
GROG! Your Highness—
GRAND D. You will return this very evening to the Court of the Elector—our future father-in-law
GROG. Eh, what?
GRAND D. And you will inform him of my happiness—for is it not happiness to be united to Prince Paul
PRINCE P. Oh! oh!
GRAND D. Well, we must bend to our fate. When we can't have what we like, we must like what we have

GENERAL BOOM.

At last I remount the tall feather!

PUCK.

At last I'm to power restored!

PRINCE PAUL.

At last we're bound in Hymen's tether!

GROG.

At last I see my little ones ador'd!

WANDA.

To our cot dearest now return we.

FRITZ.

At home we shall be on safe ground

GRAND DUCHESS.

Come, the fortune of war ne'er spurn we
Perhaps the bliss may there yet be found

FRITZ.

Let other battle with the foe,
I bid a long farewell to slaughter,
My patriotic zeal I'll show
By rearing many a son and daughter

CHORUS.

His patriotic zeal he'll show
By rearing many a son and daughter

GRAND DUCHESS.

Since now with more or less effect
Our part is played—we name the day, sire:
Tho' hardly dreamt—'tis most correct—
So drops the curtain on our play, sirs

CHORUS.

Tho' hardly dreamt—'tis most correct,
So drops the curtain on our play, sirs.

GRAND DUCHESS.

Oh how my sire hath hail'd the sight—
His daughter settled down outright?

CHORUS.

Ah! how her sire hath hail'd the sight—
His daughter settled down outright.

FINIS